How To Draw Realistic Skulls Volume 5

Simple Guide to Drawing Skulls

How to Draw Skulls

By : Gala Publication

Published By :

Gala Publication

© Copyright 2015 – Gala Publication

ISBN-13: **978-1522785866**
ISBN-10: **1522785868**

Table of Contents

4

ANGRY BIRD
SKULL

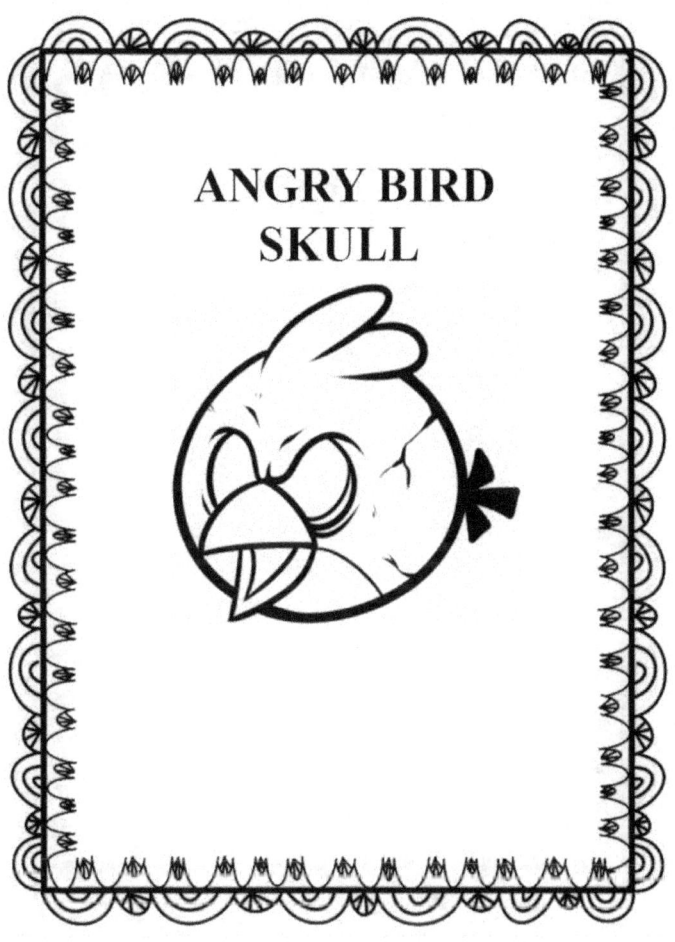

STEP 1

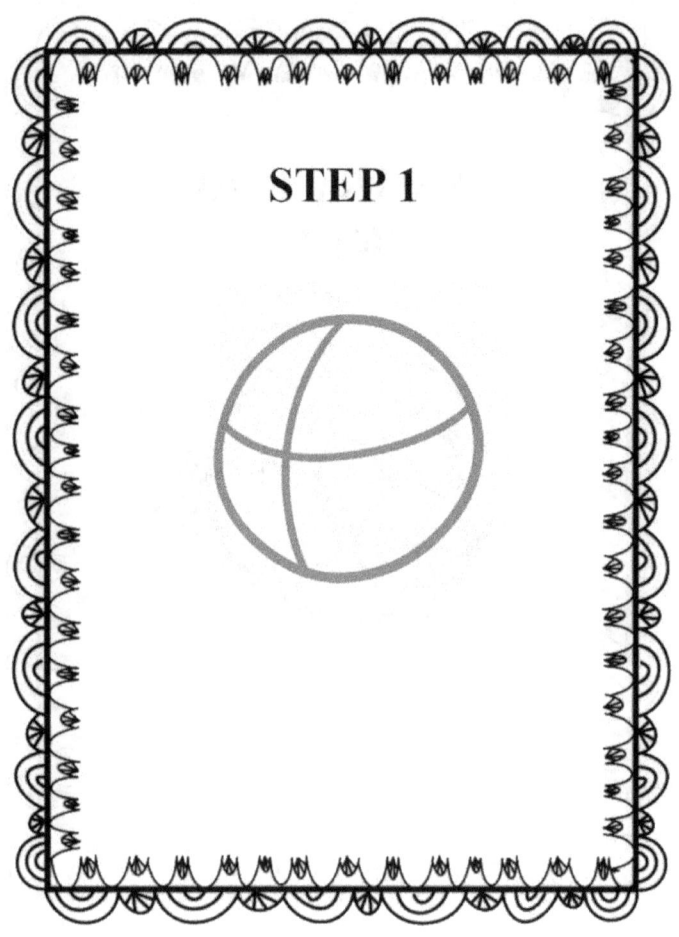

STEP 2

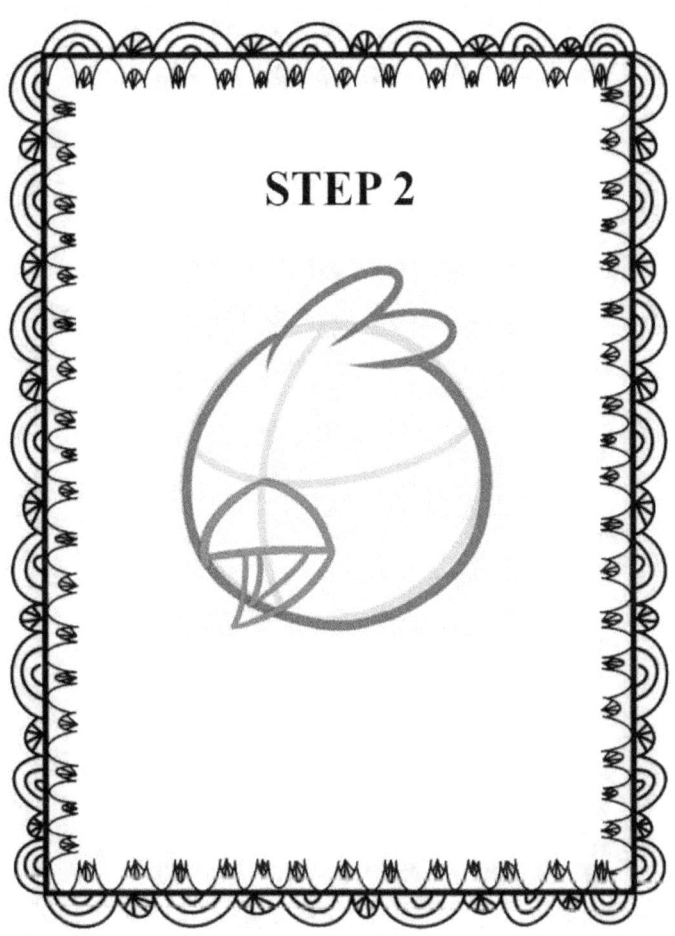

STEP 3

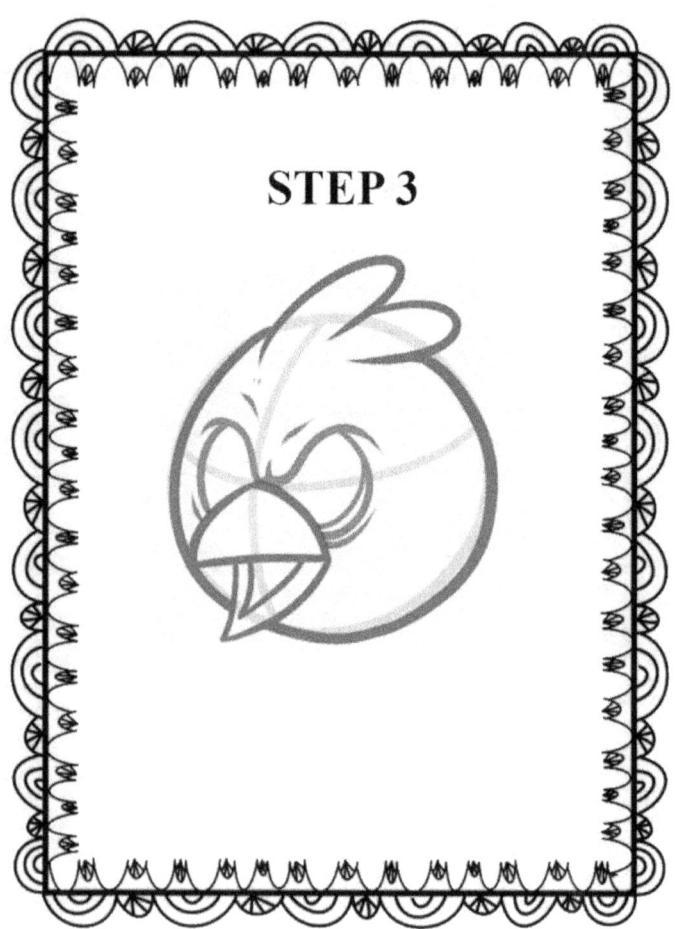

STEP 4

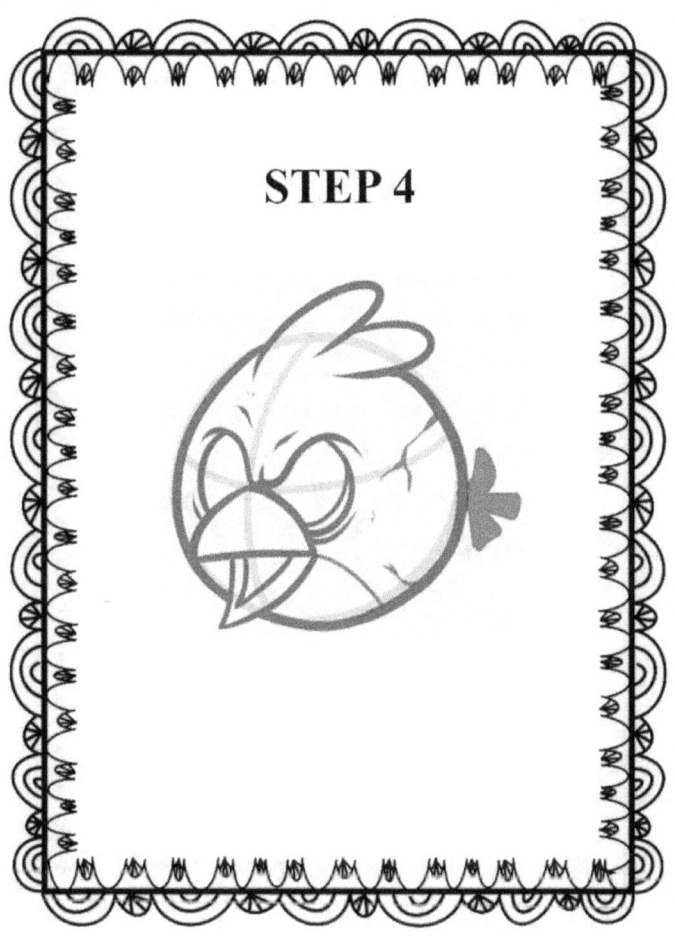

STEP 5

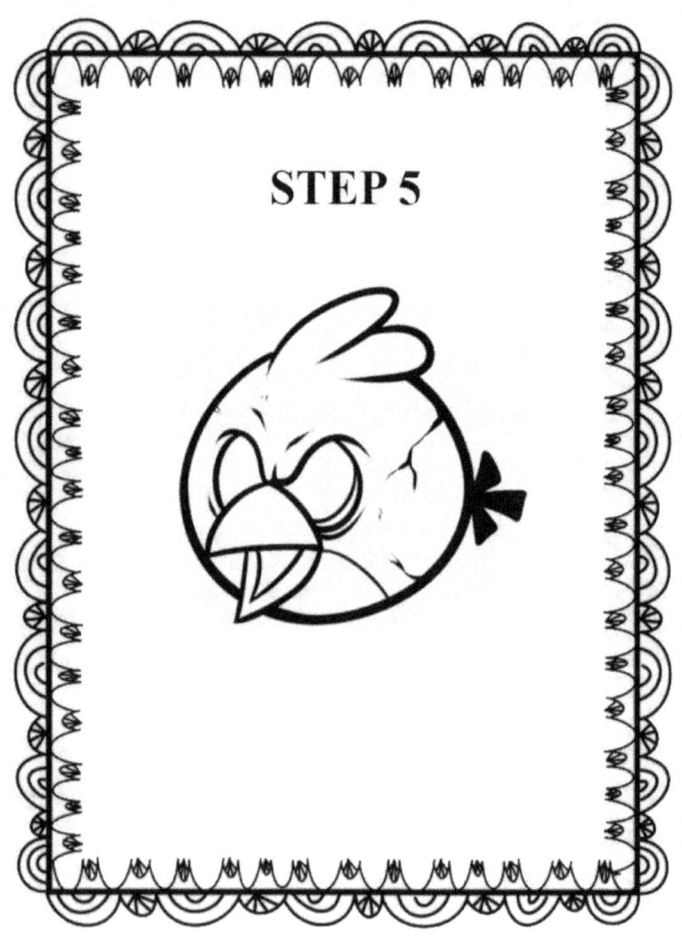

FINN SKULL

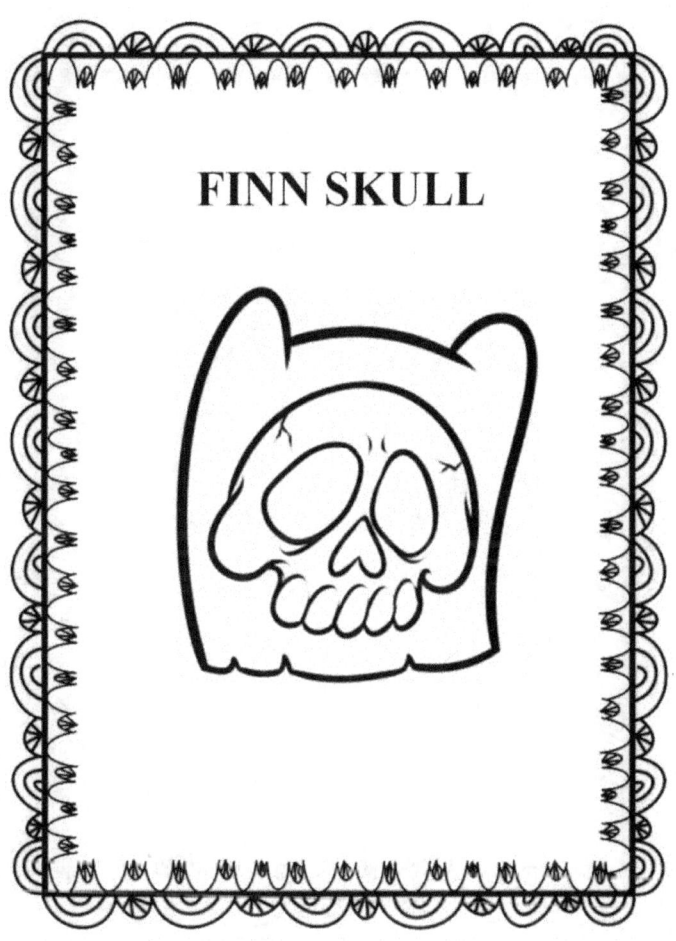

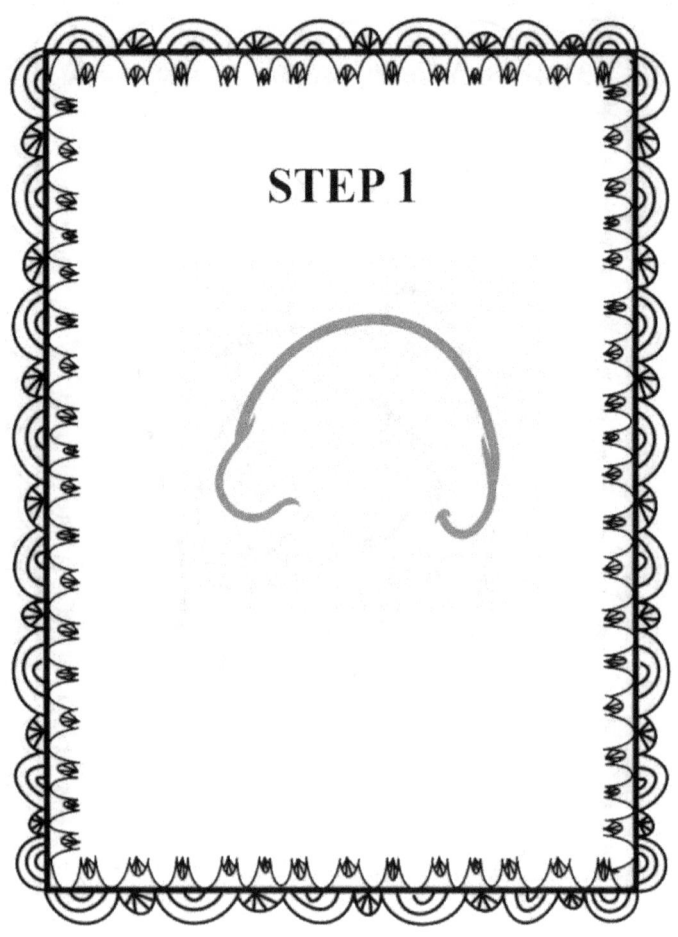

STEP 1

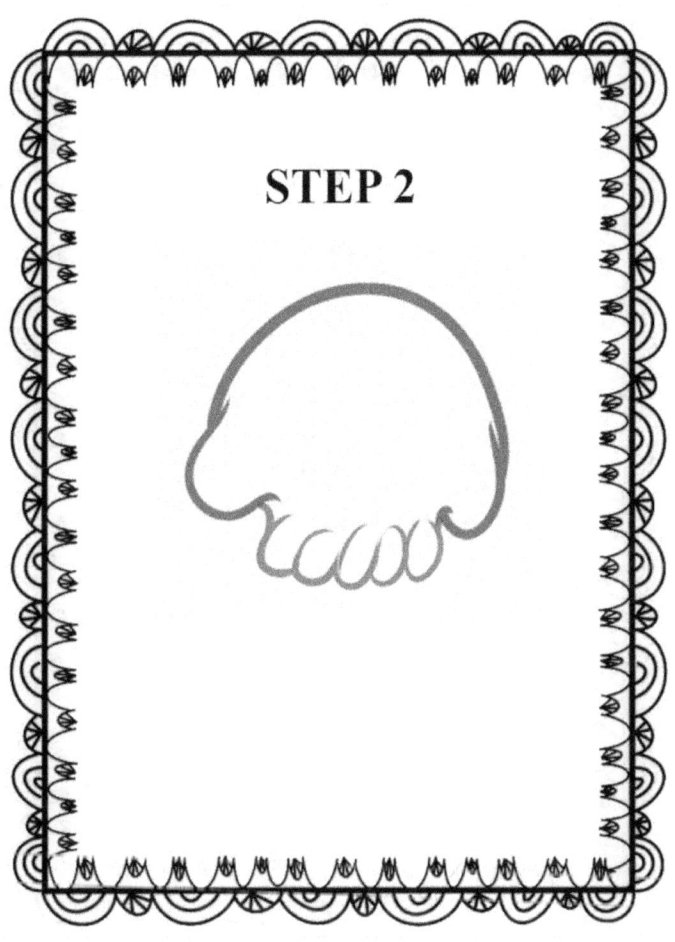

STEP 2

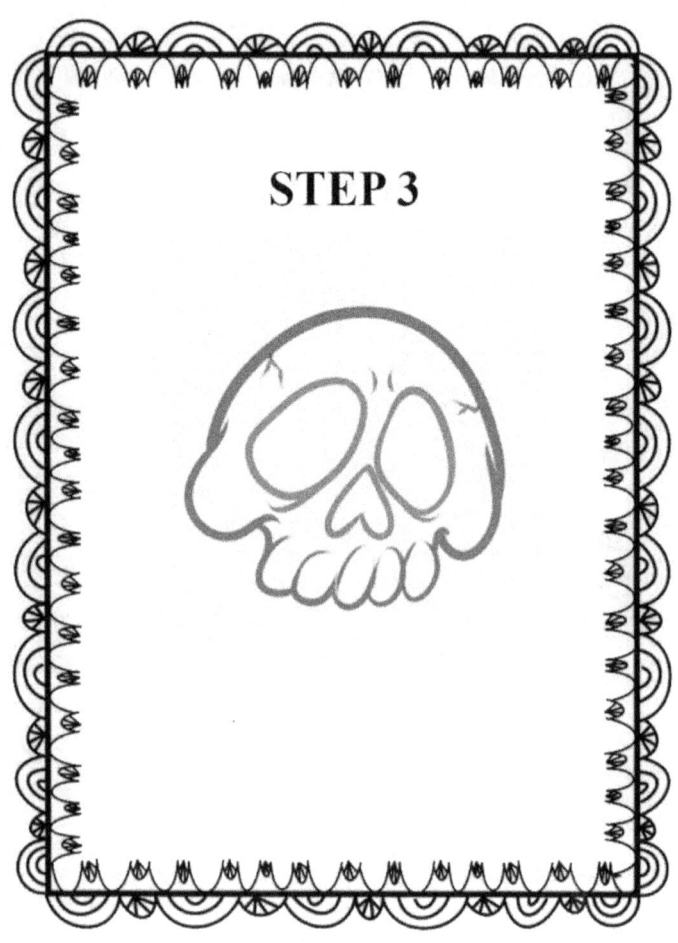

STEP 3

STEP 4

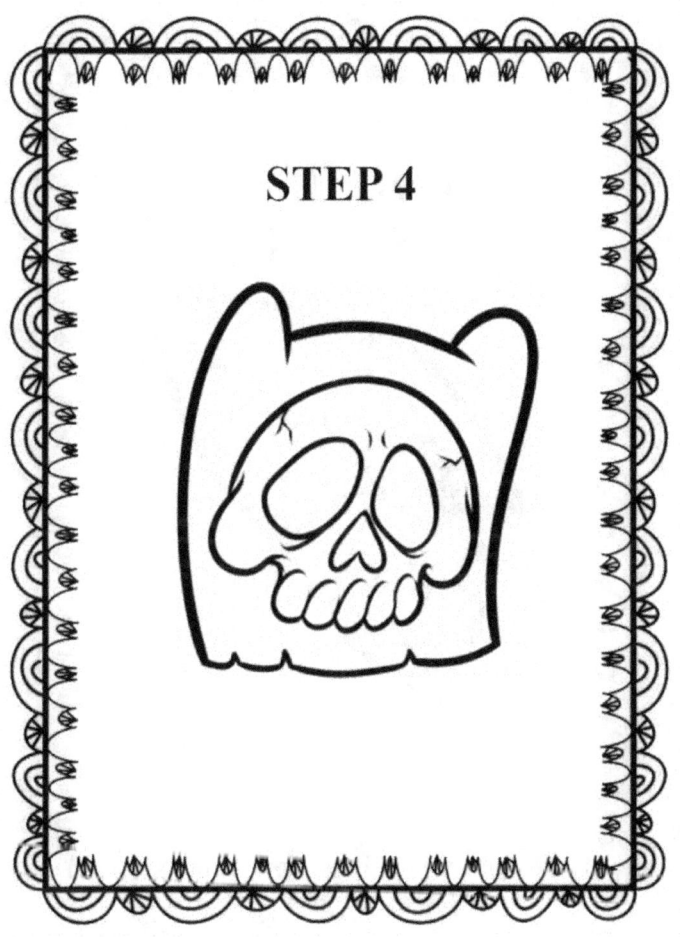

FOOTBALL
SKULL

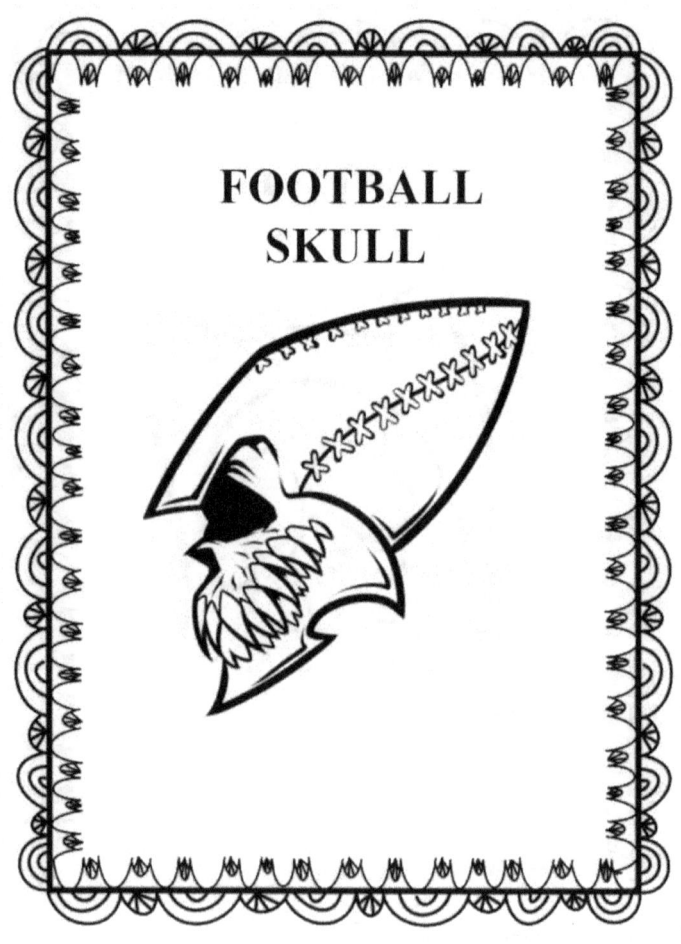

STEP 1

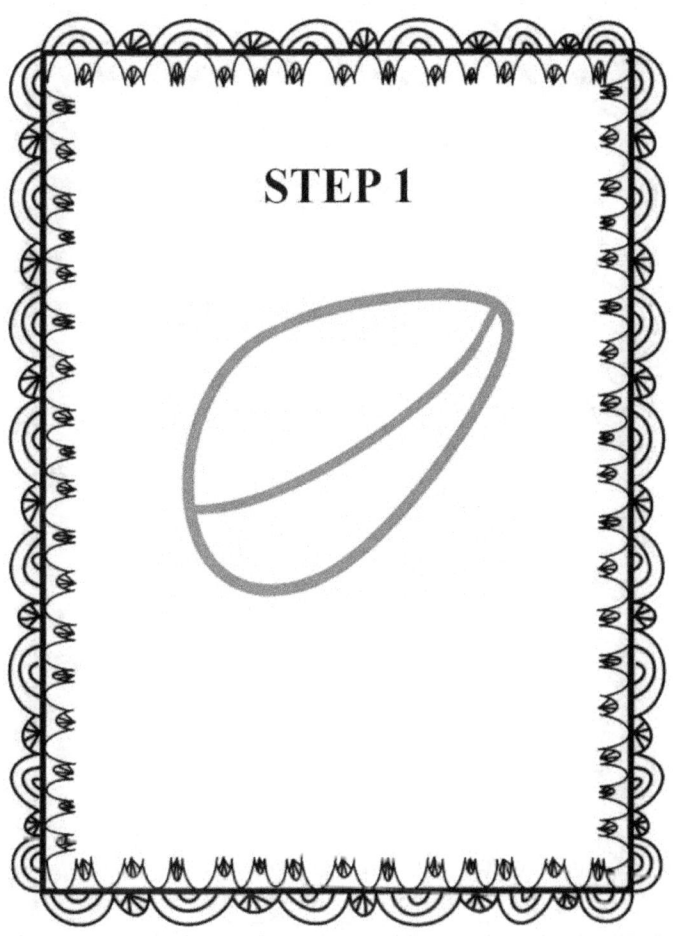

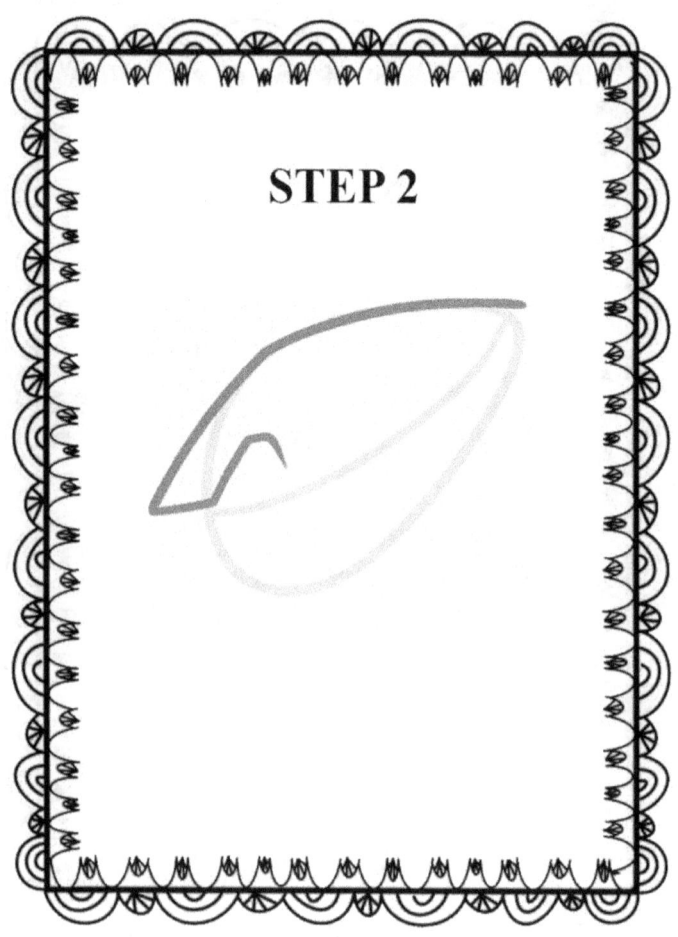

STEP 2

STEP 3

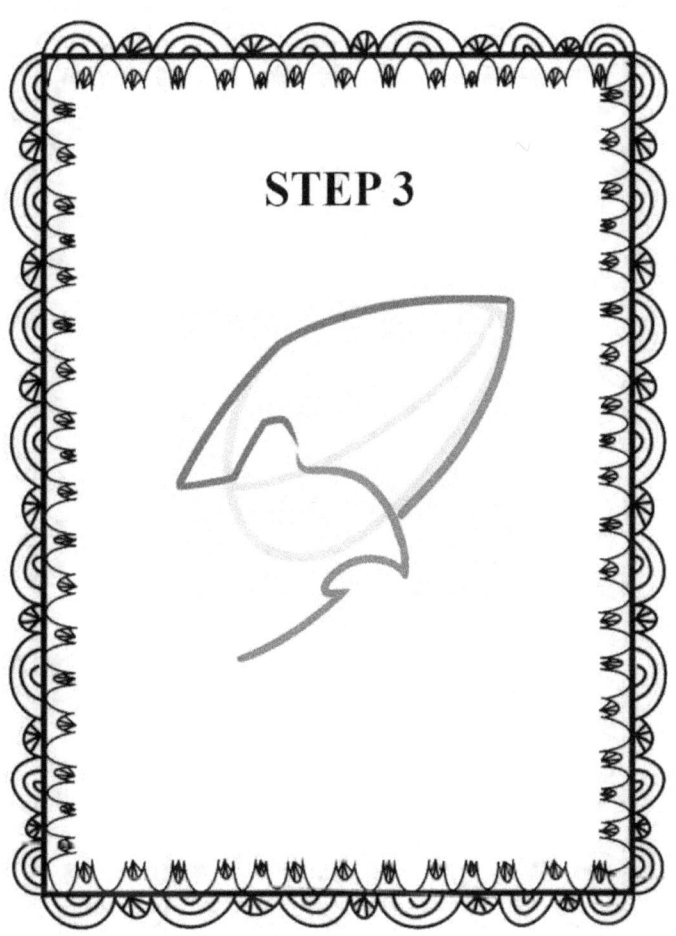

STEP 4

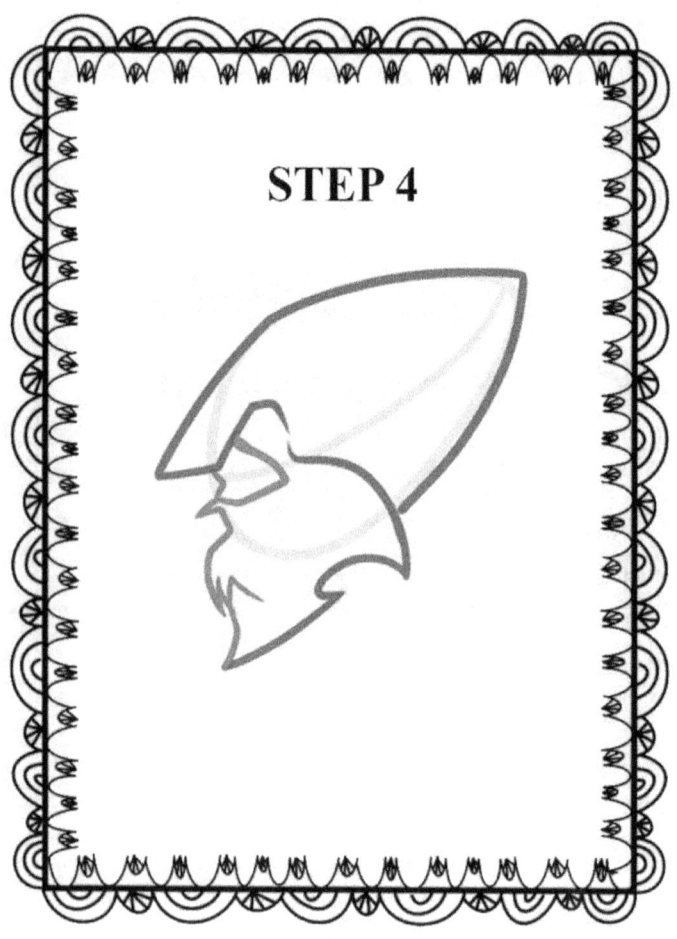

STEP 5

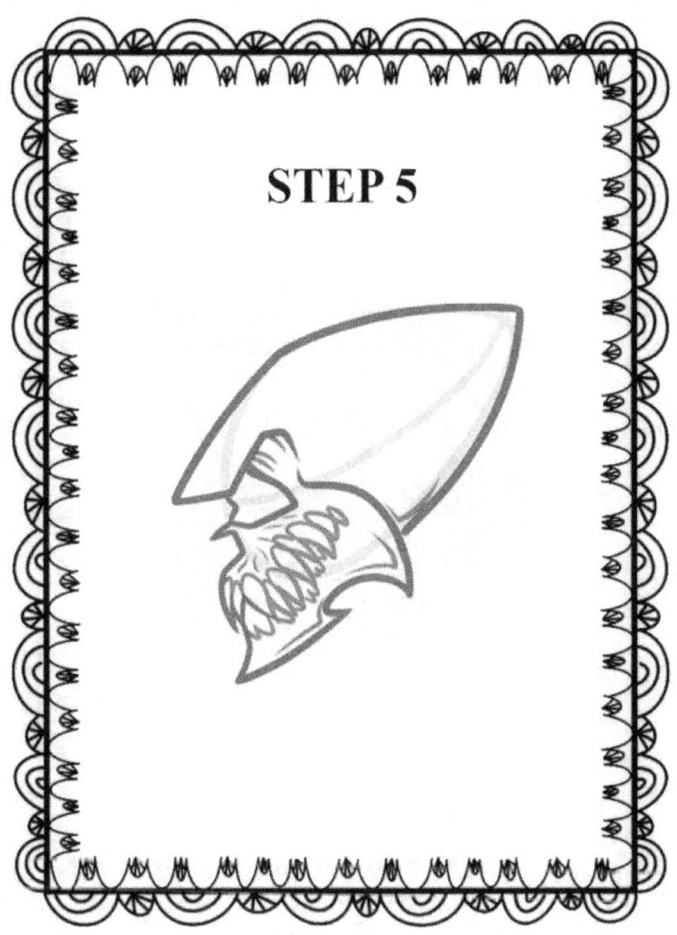

STEP 6

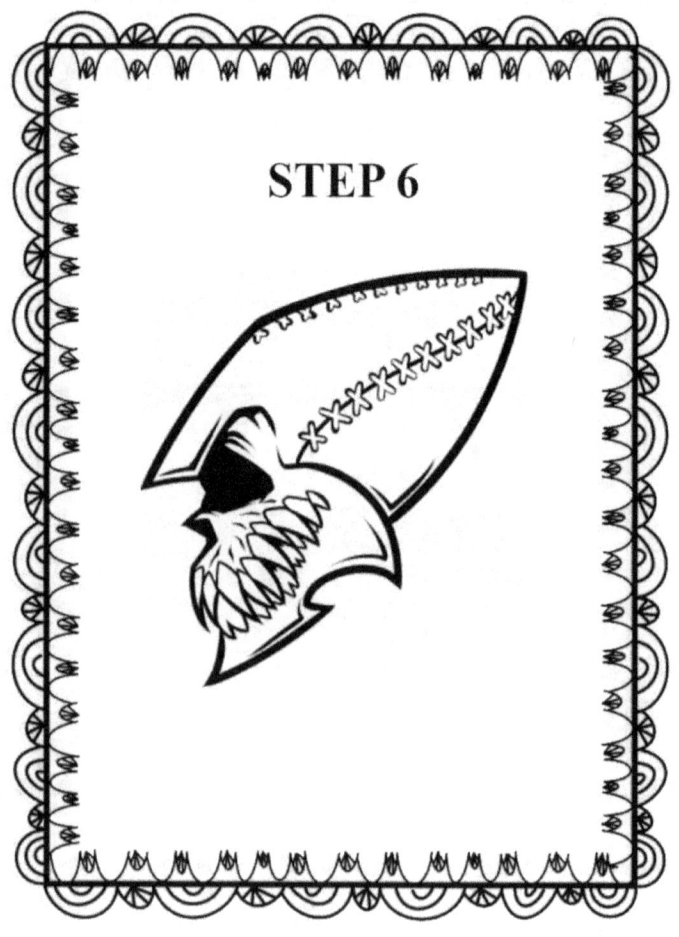

JOKER SKULL

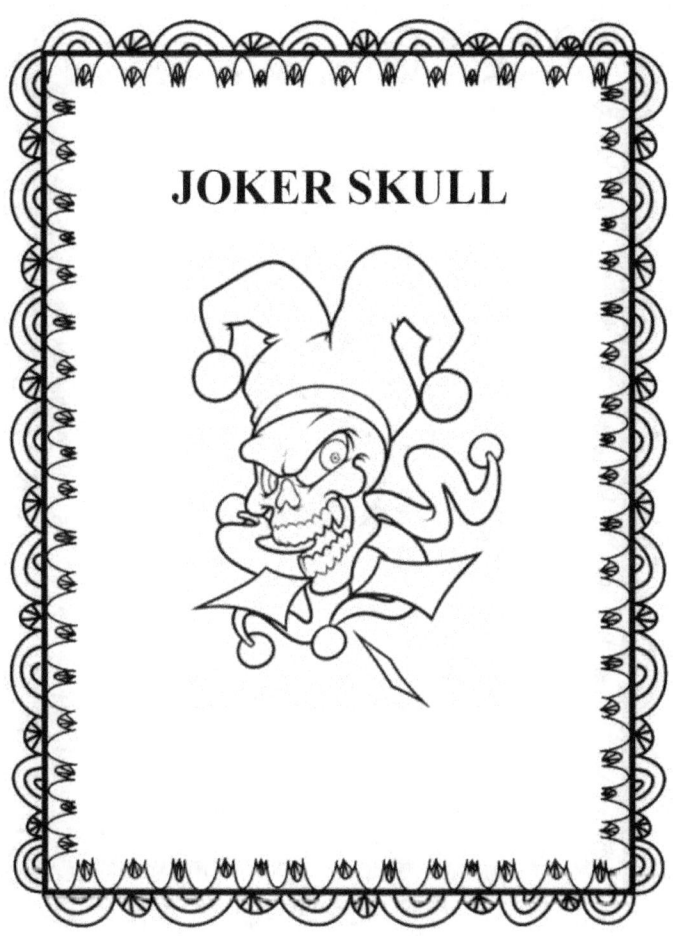

STEP 1

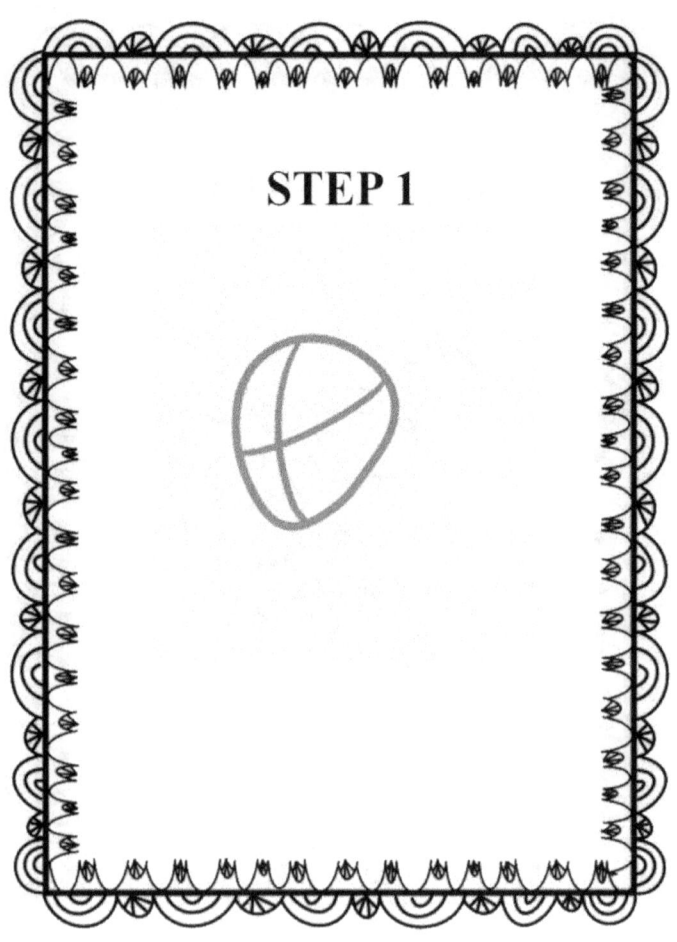

STEP 2

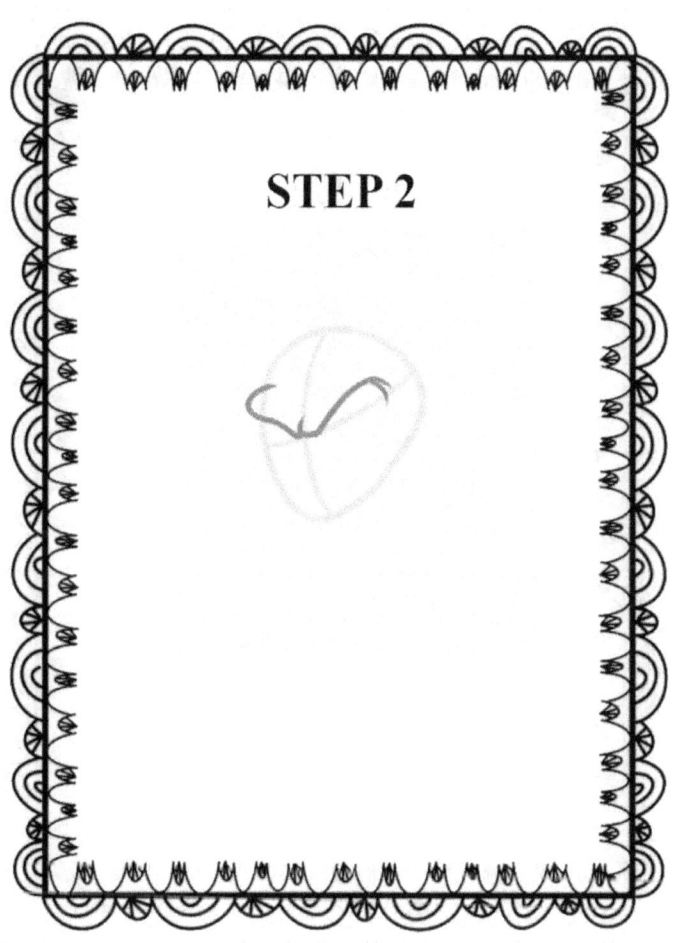

STEP 3

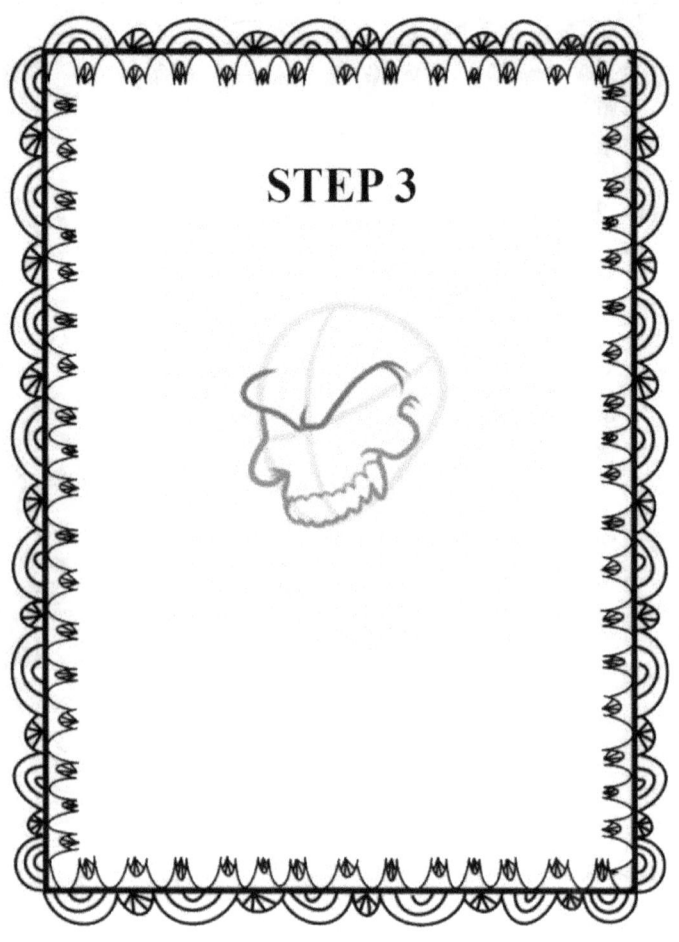

STEP 4

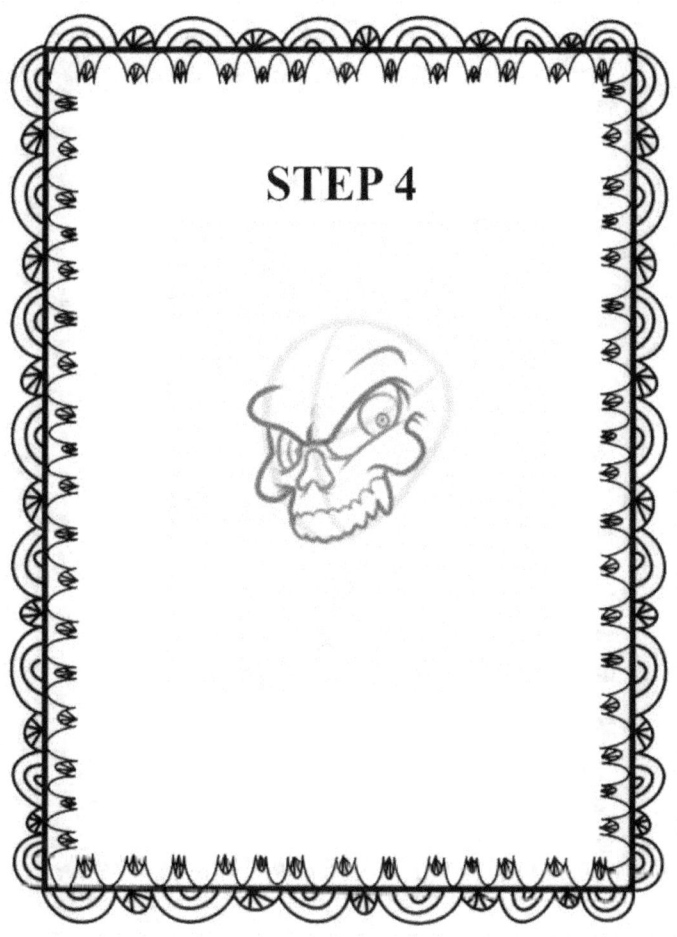

STEP 5

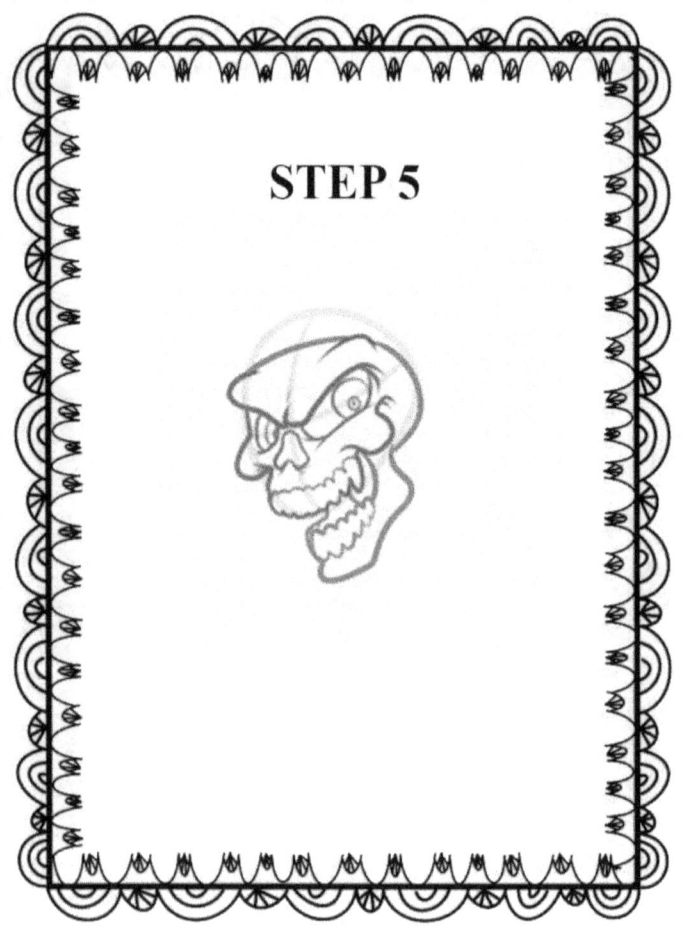

STEP 6

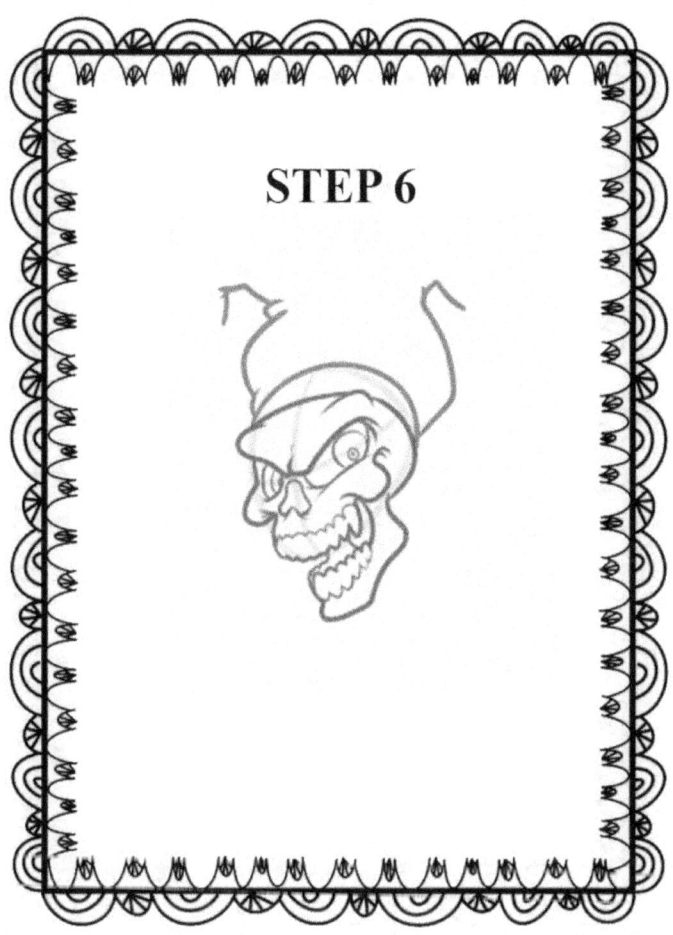

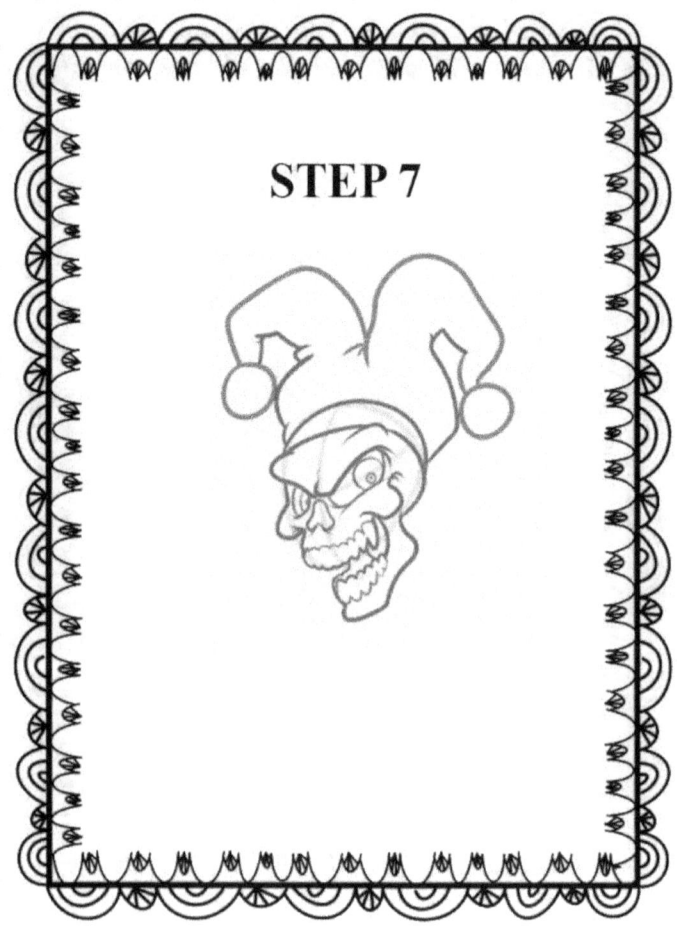

STEP 7

STEP 8

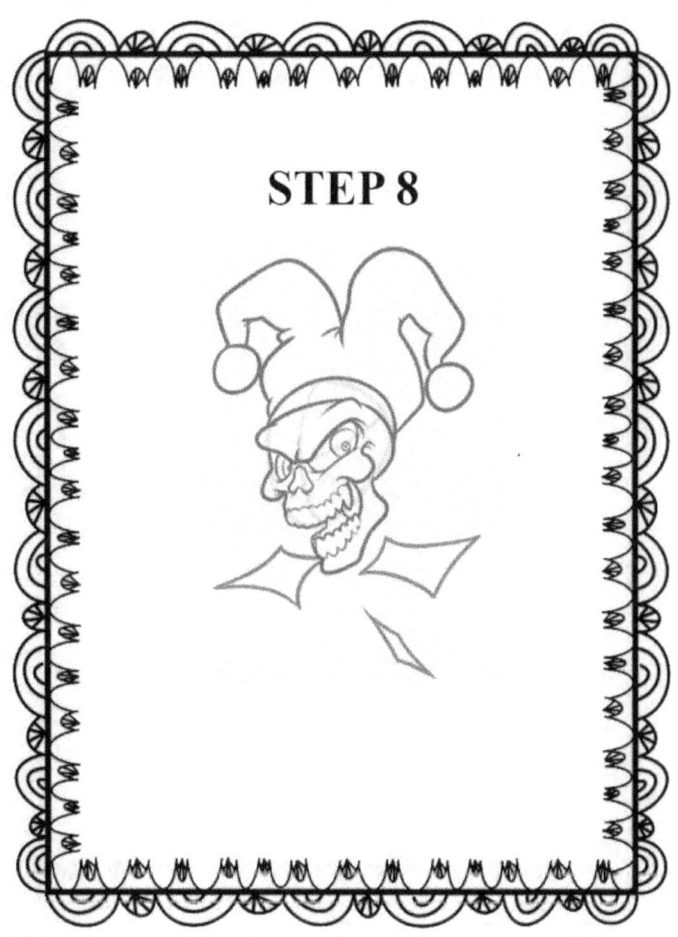

32

STEP 9

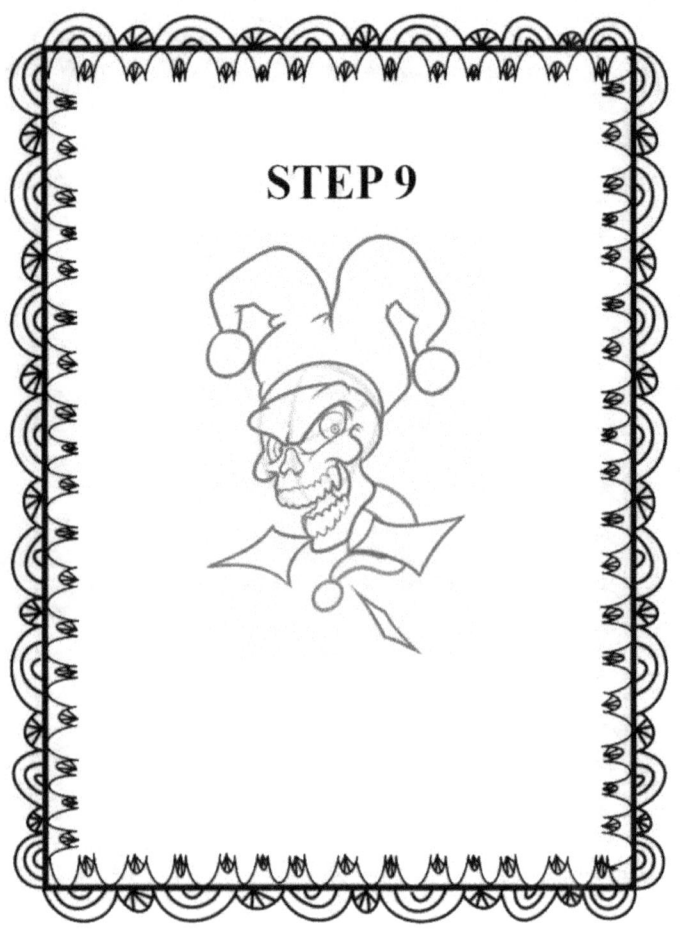

33

STEP 10

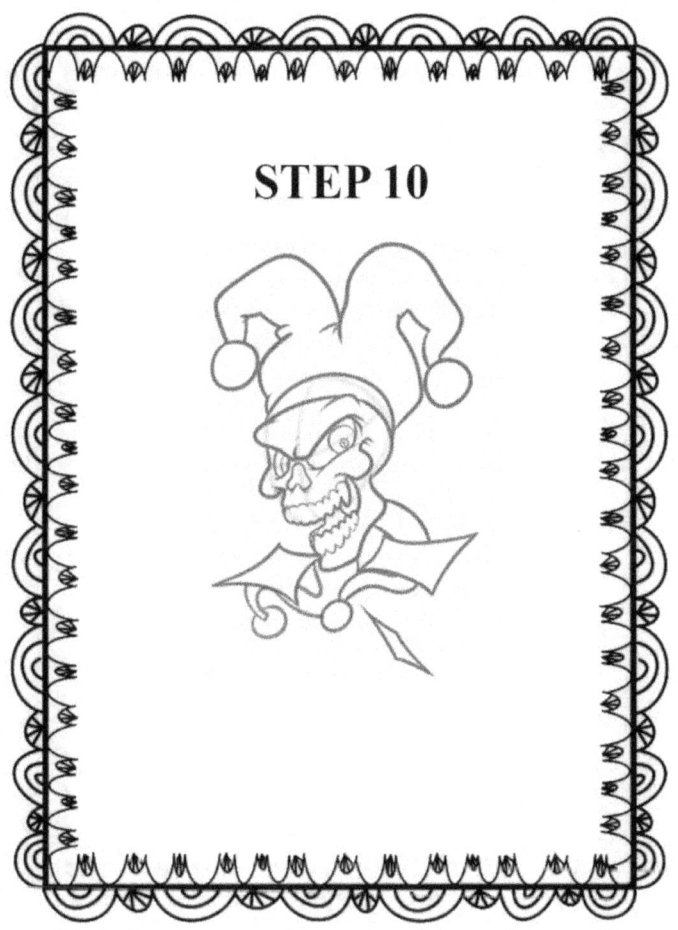

STEP 11

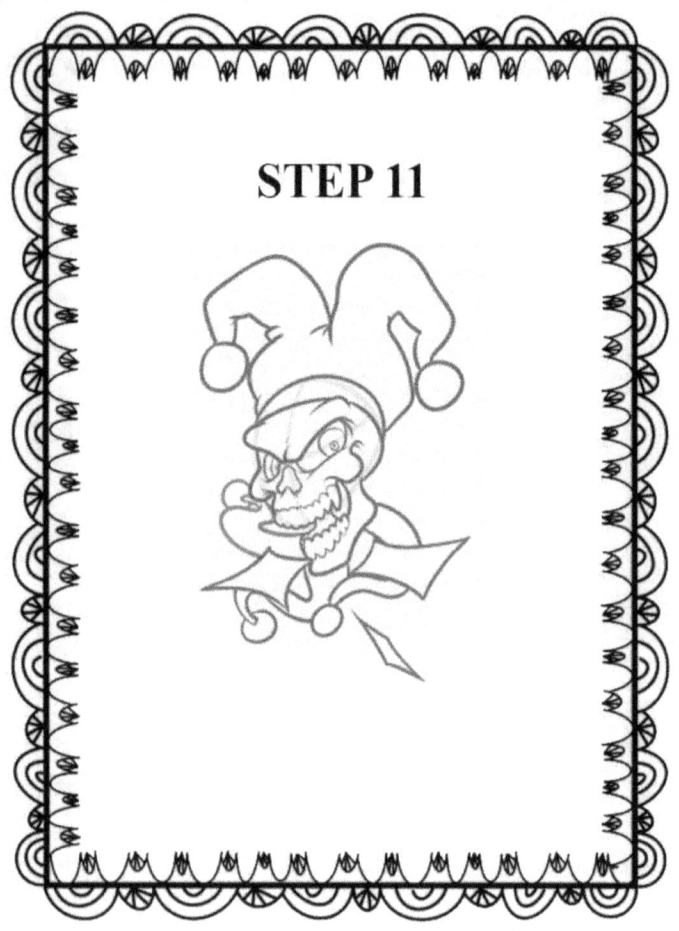

STEP 12

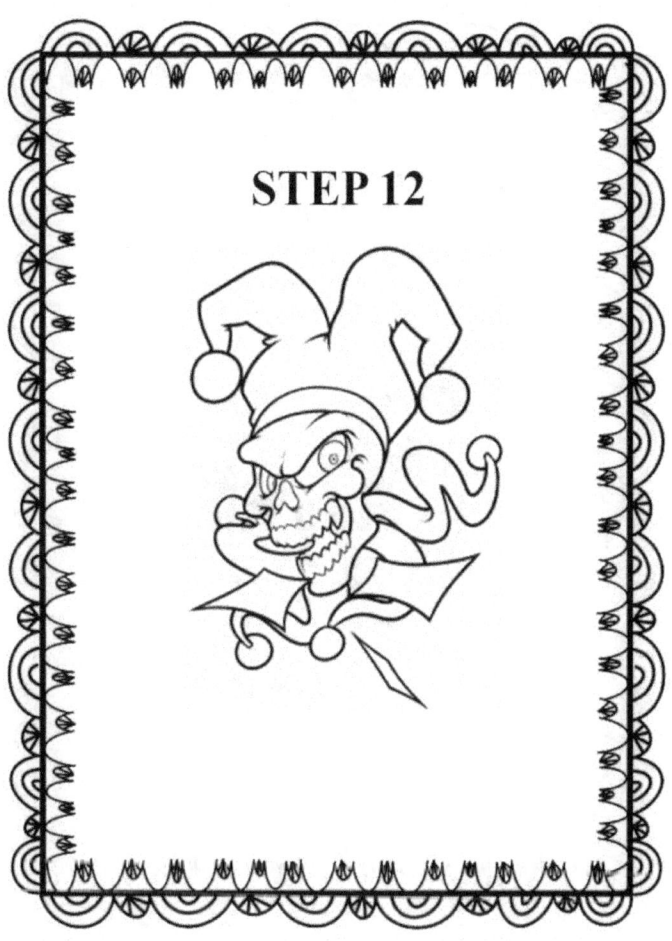

MILITRY SKULL

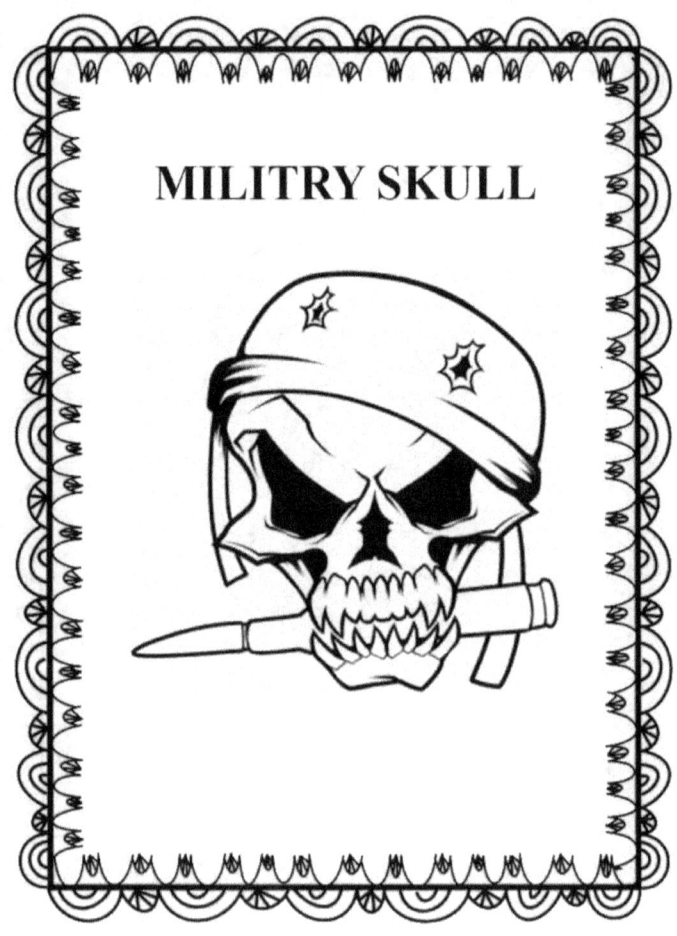

STEP 1

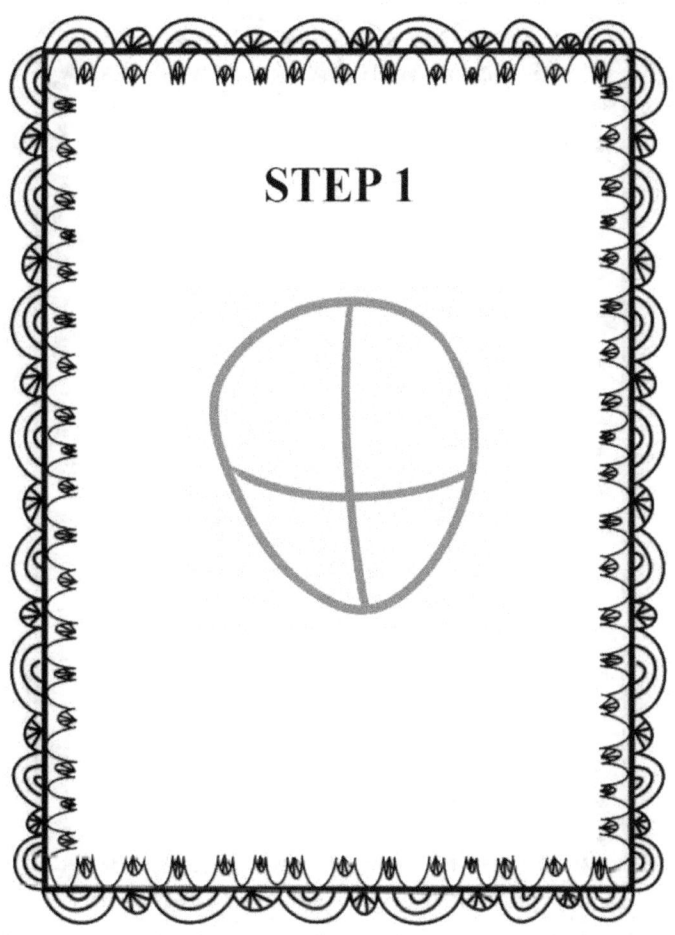

STEP 2

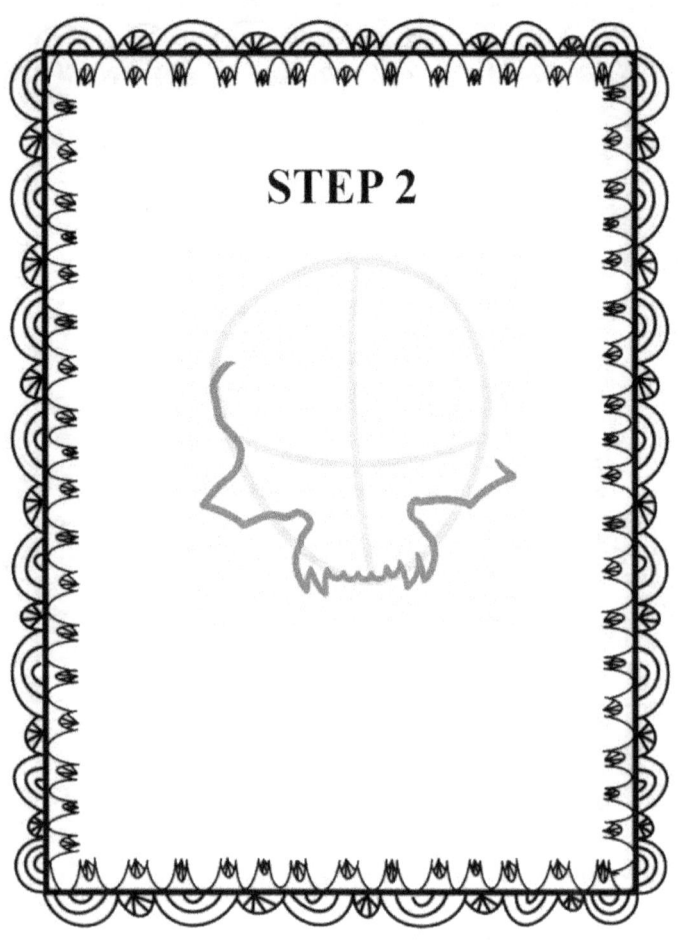

STEP 3

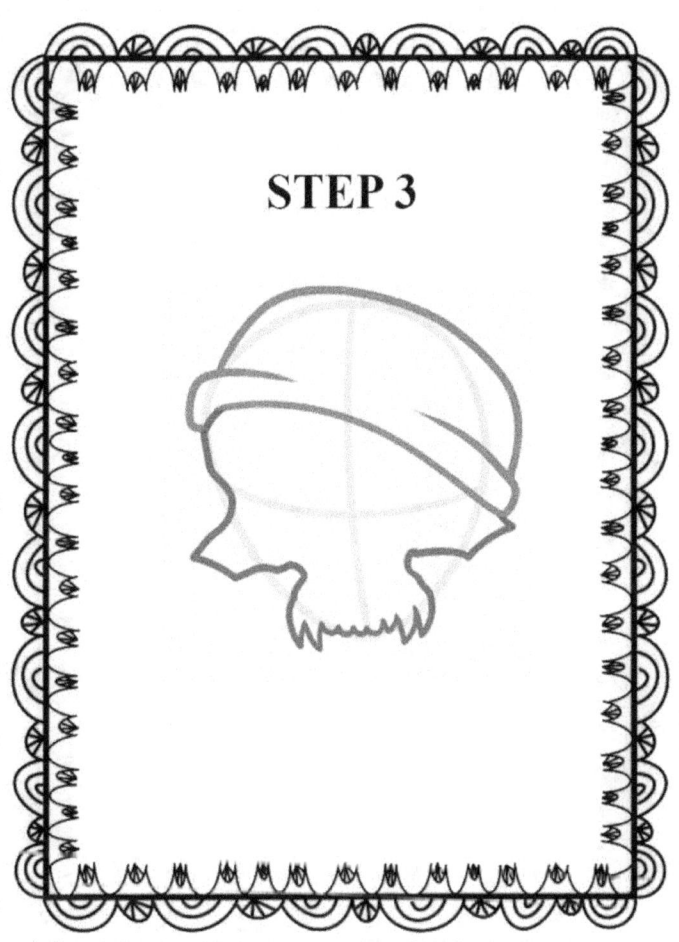

STEP 4

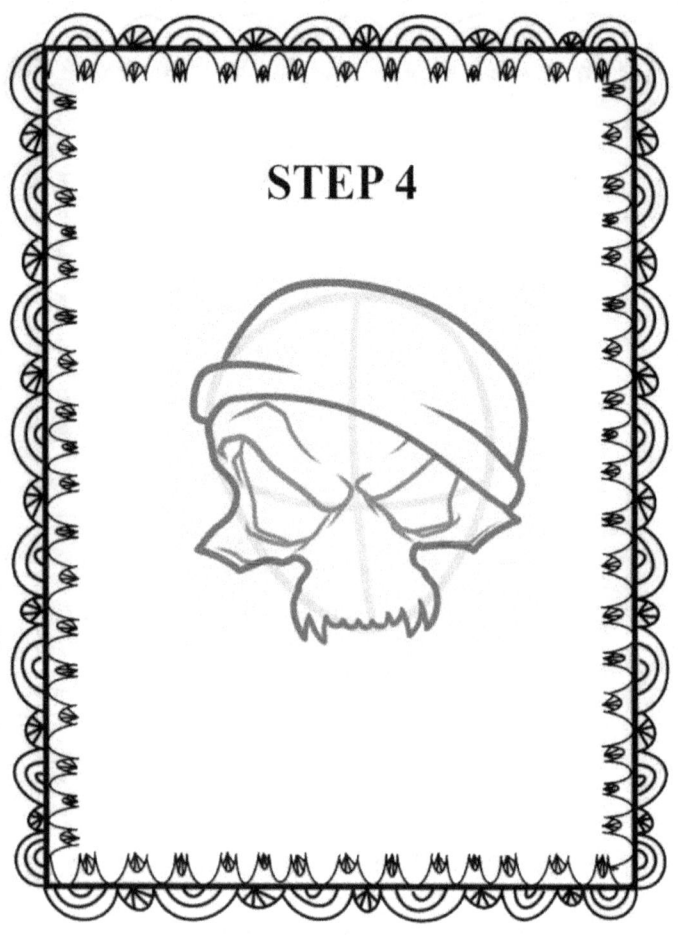

STEP 5

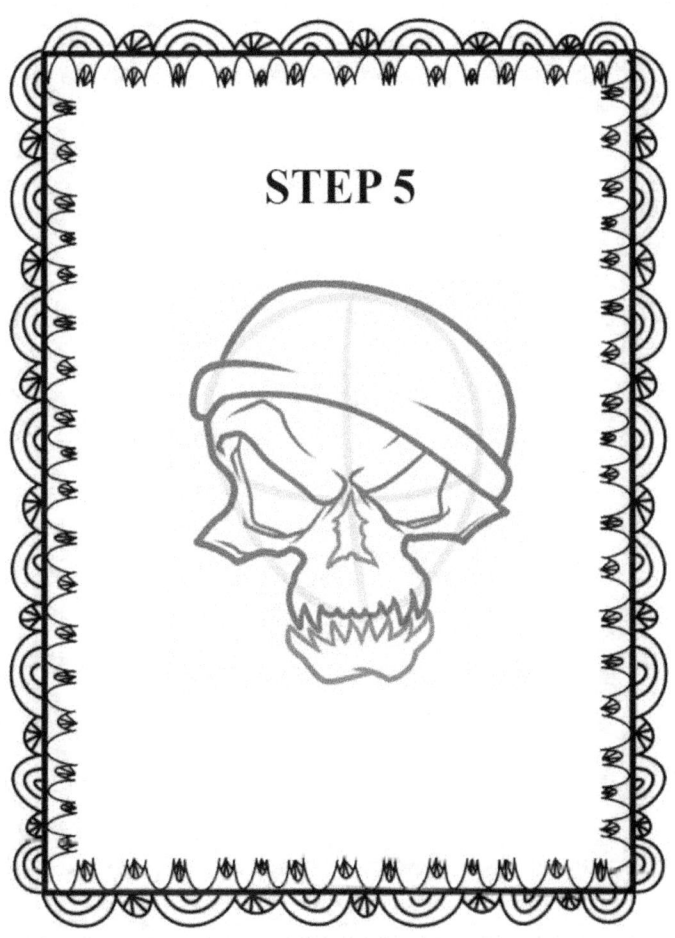

STEP 6

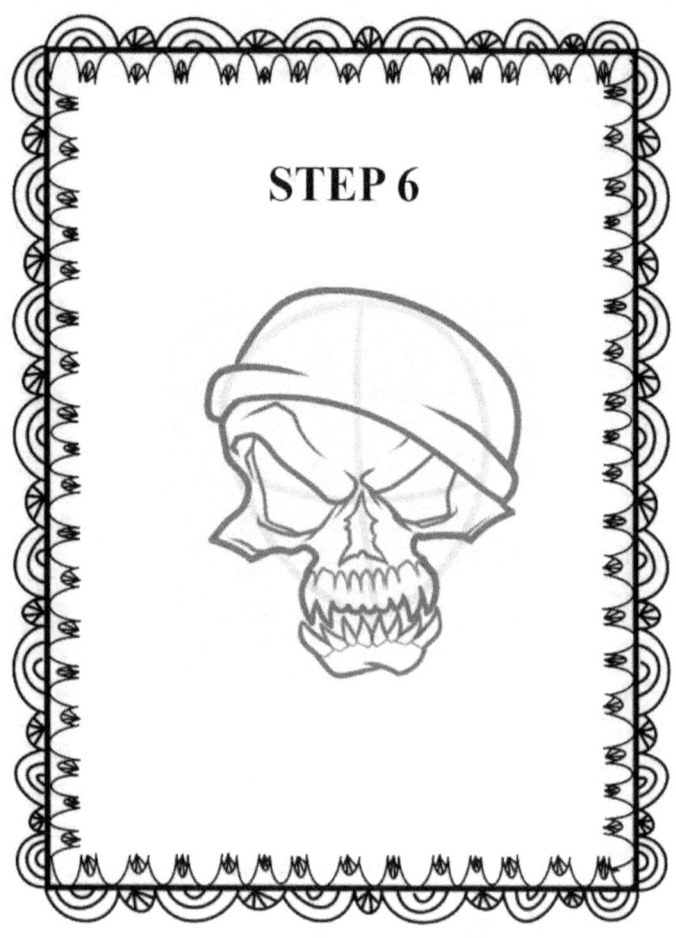

STEP 7

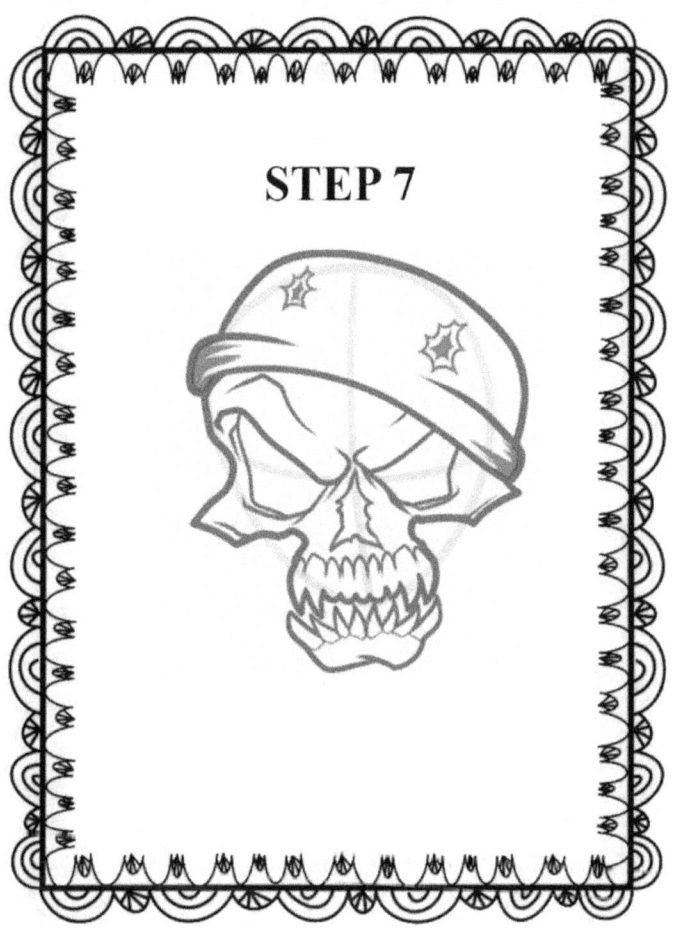

STEP 8

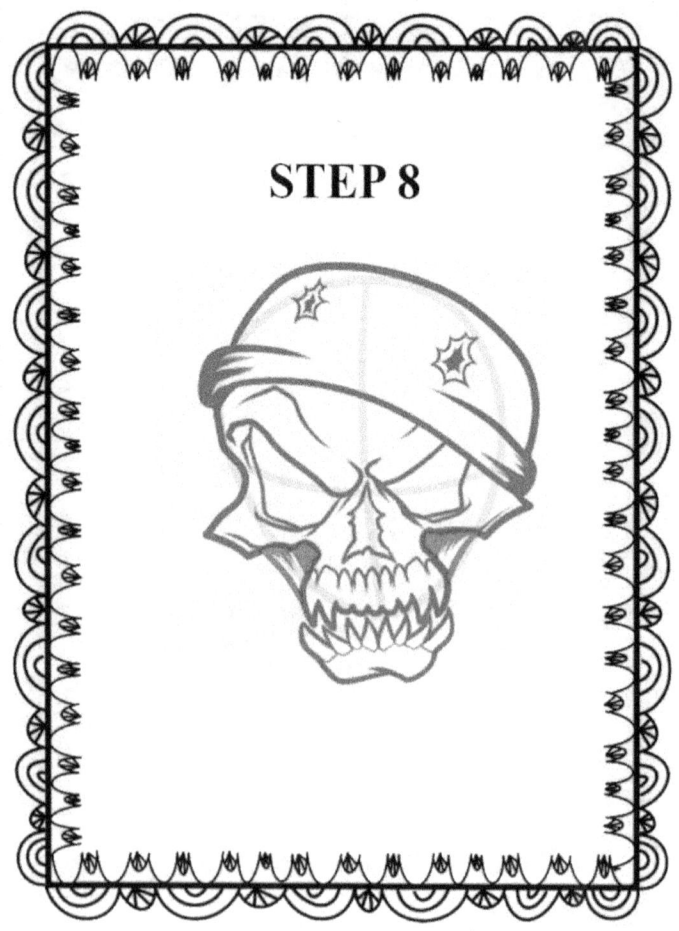

STEP 9

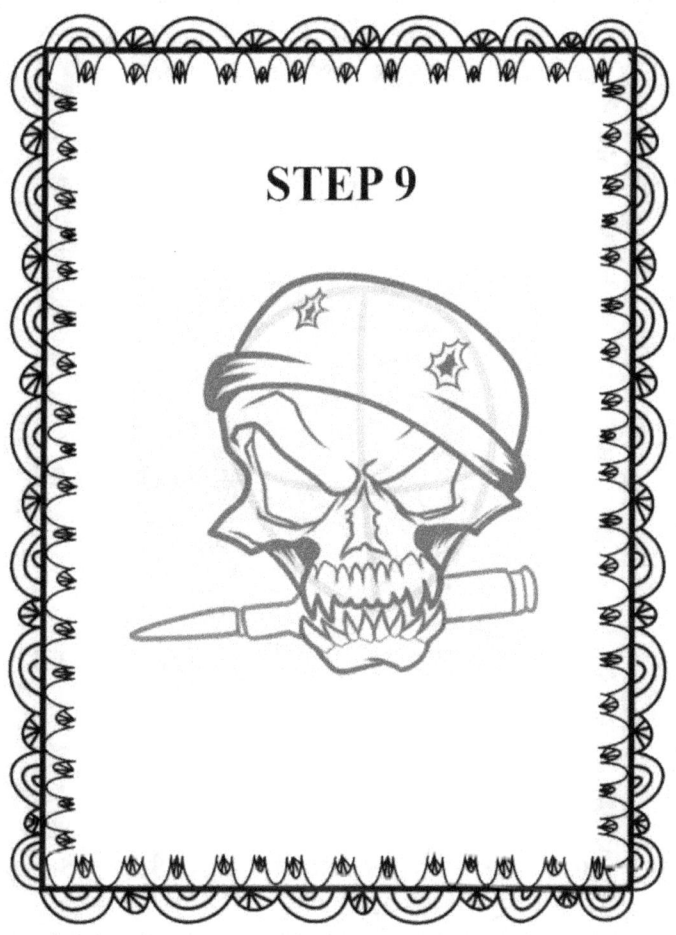

STEP 10

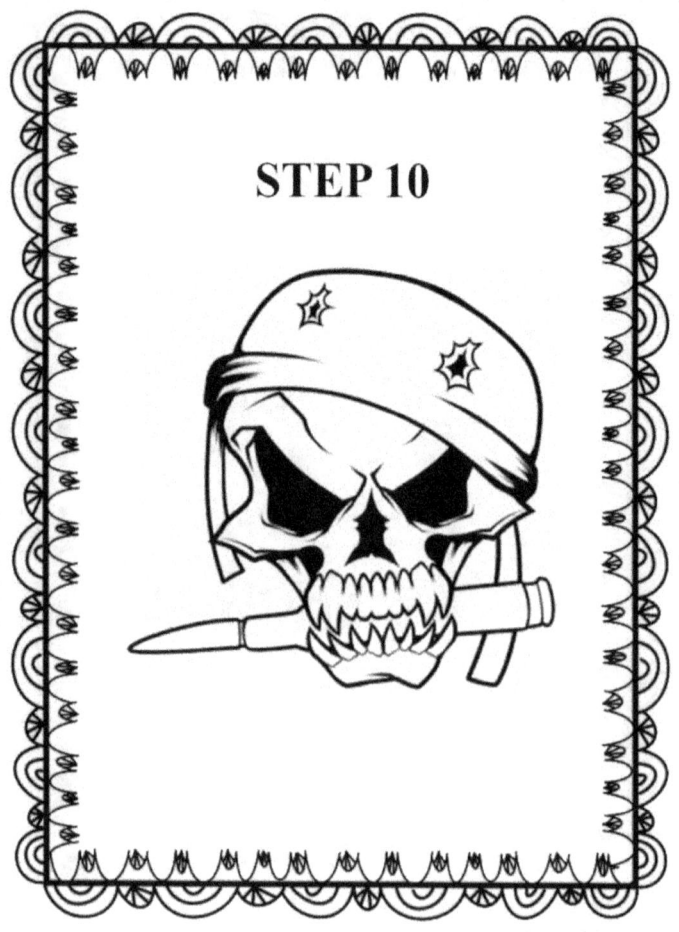

MONROE SKULL

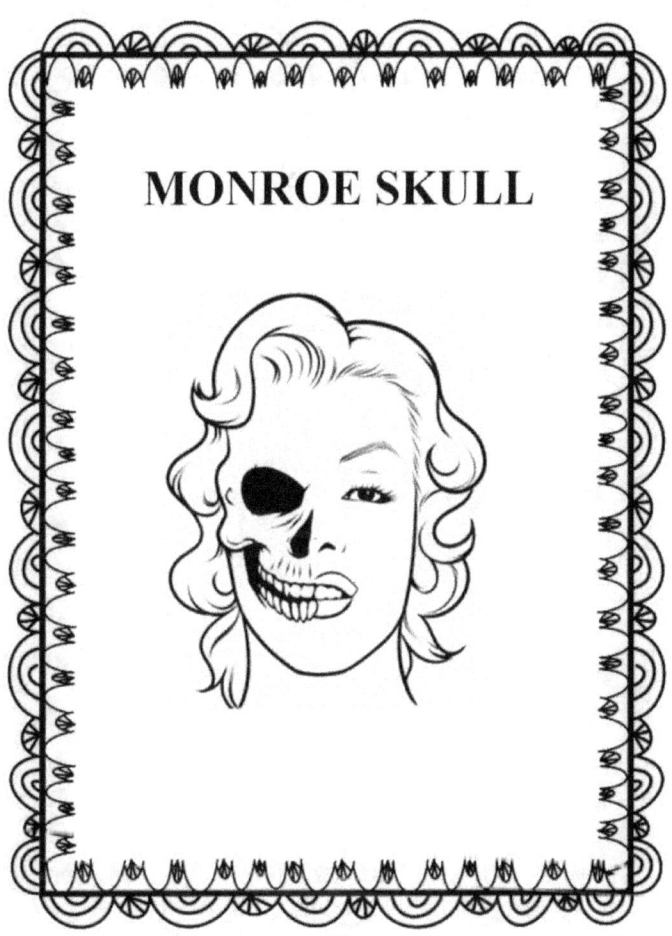

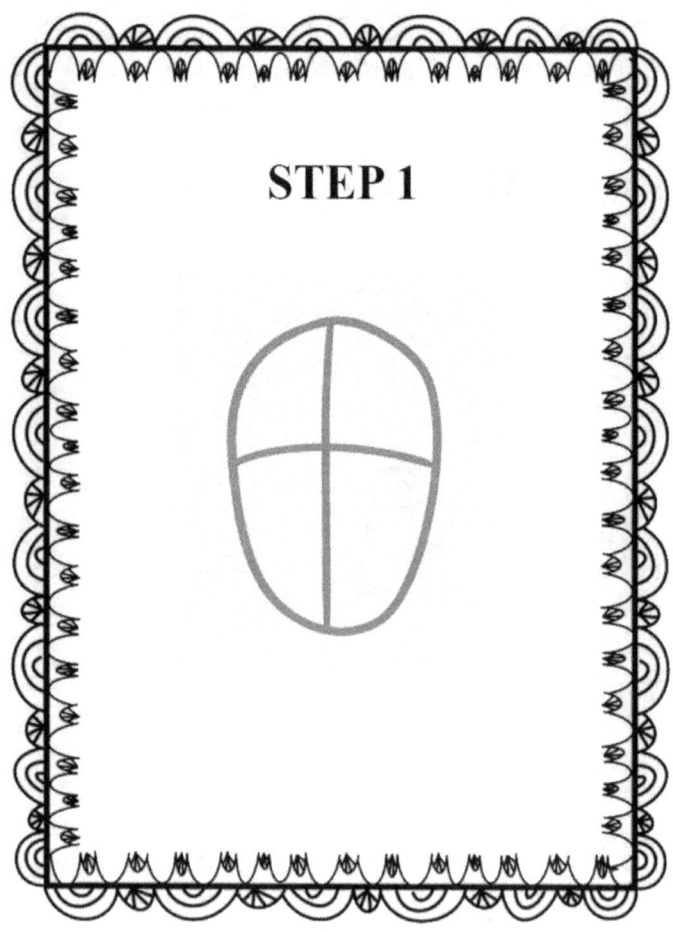

STEP 1

STEP 2

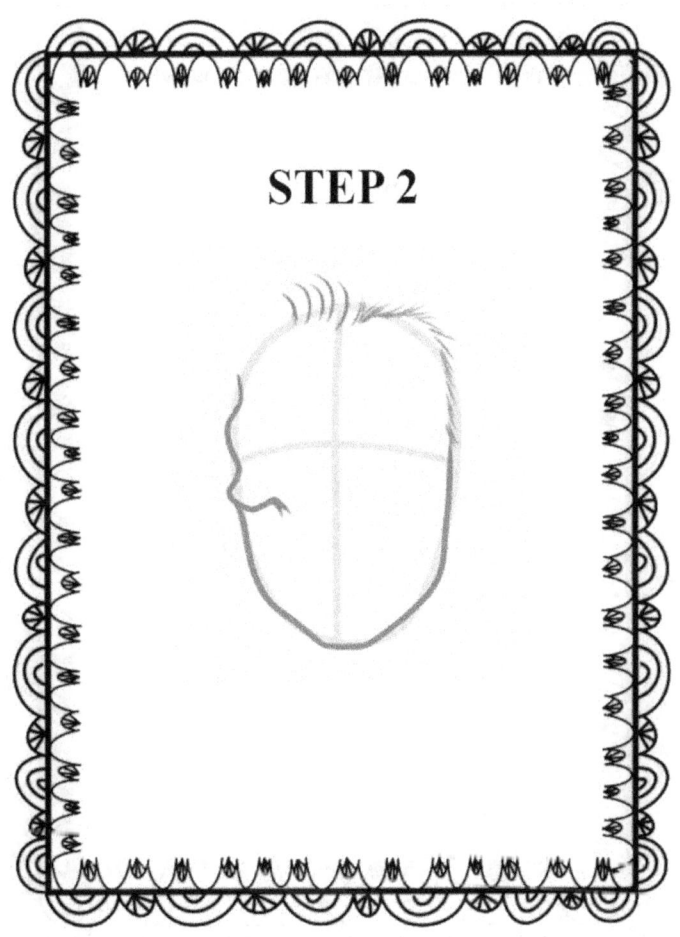

STEP 3

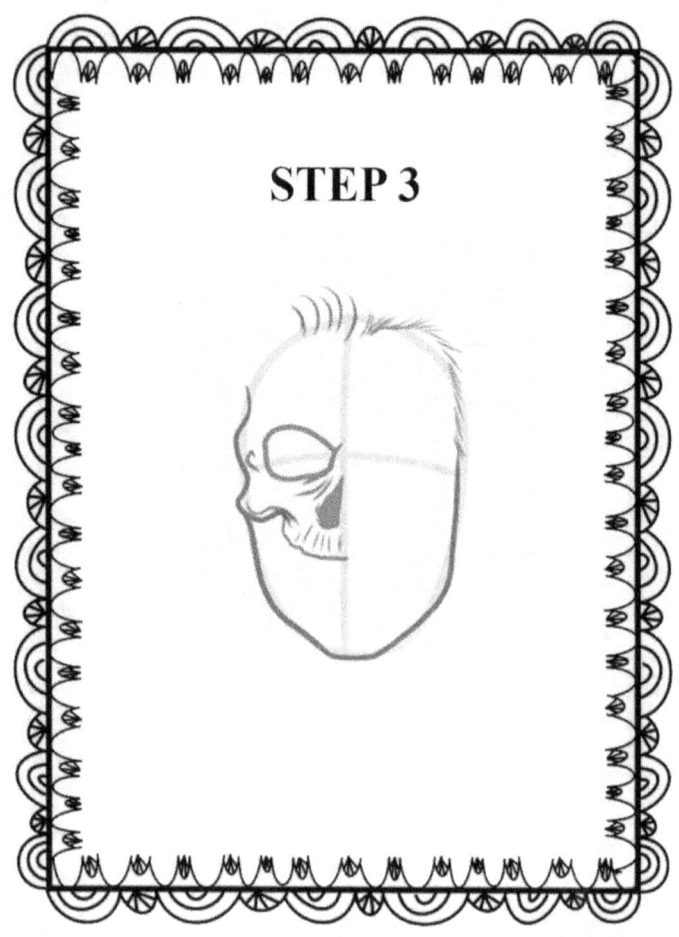

STEP 4

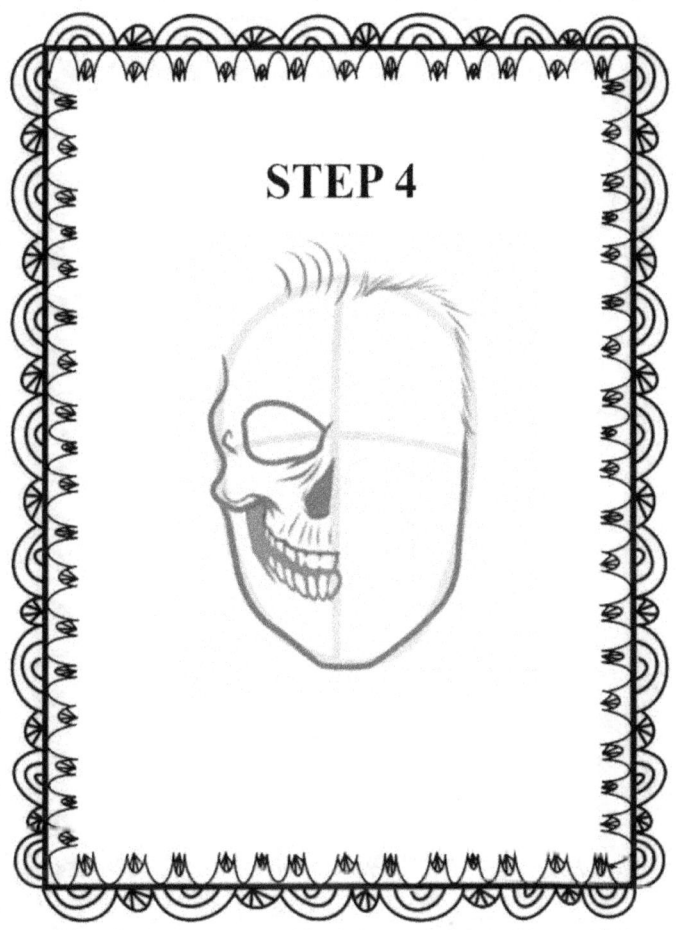

STEP 5

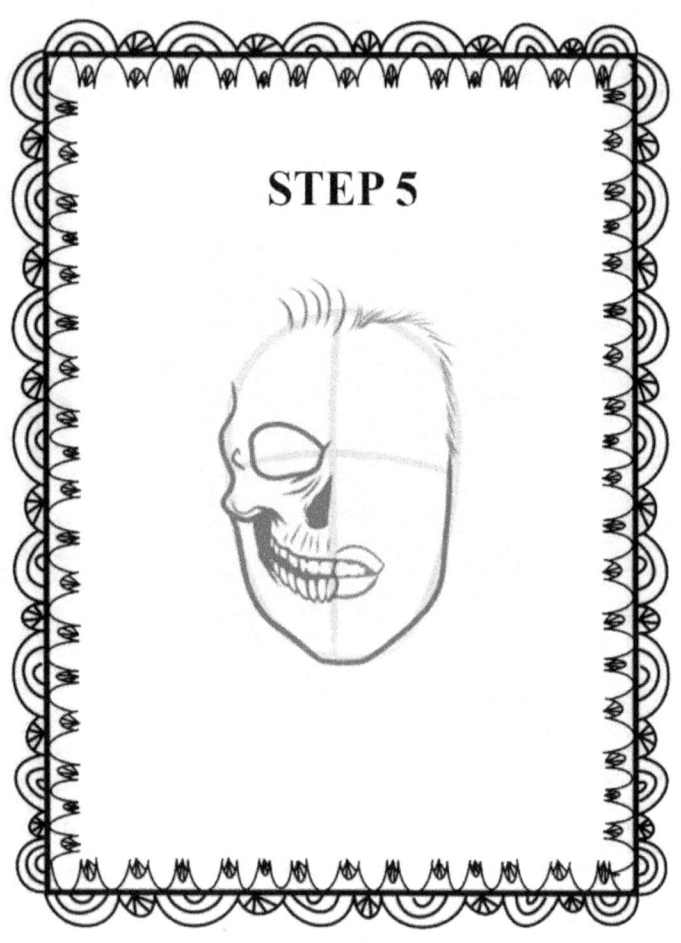

STEP 6

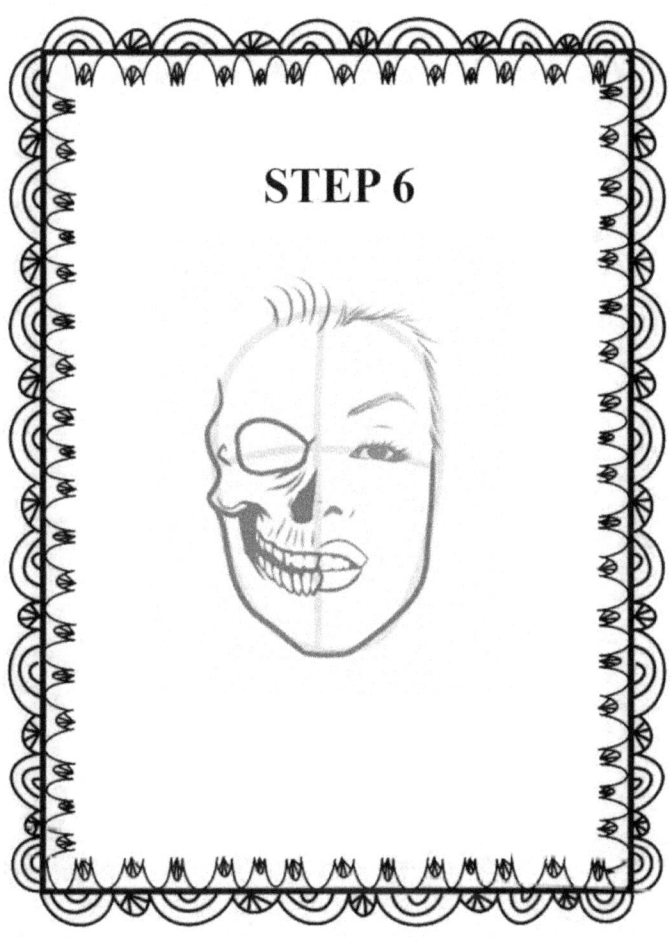

STEP 7

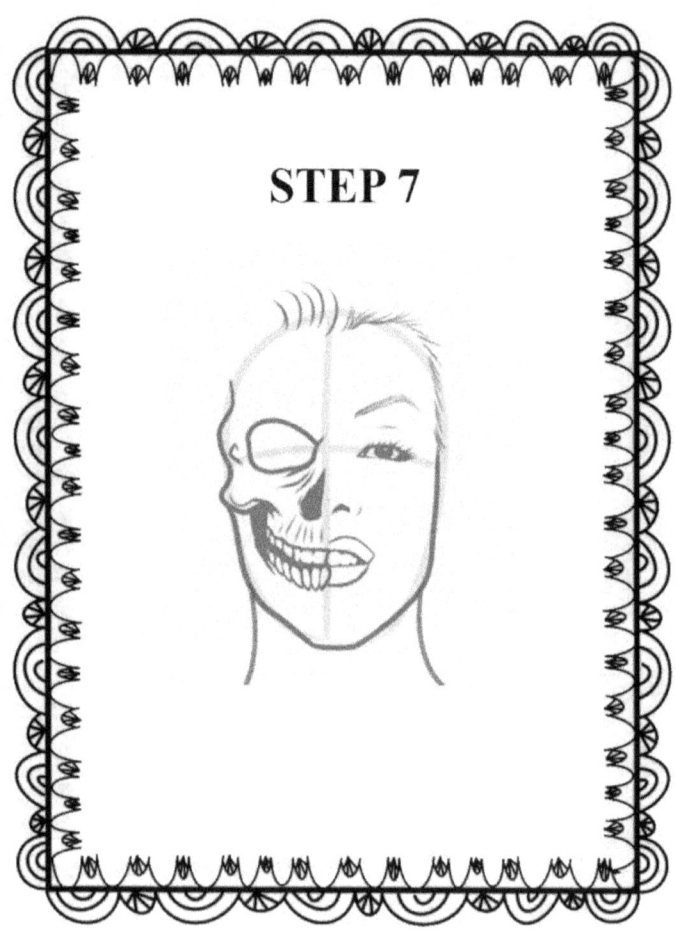

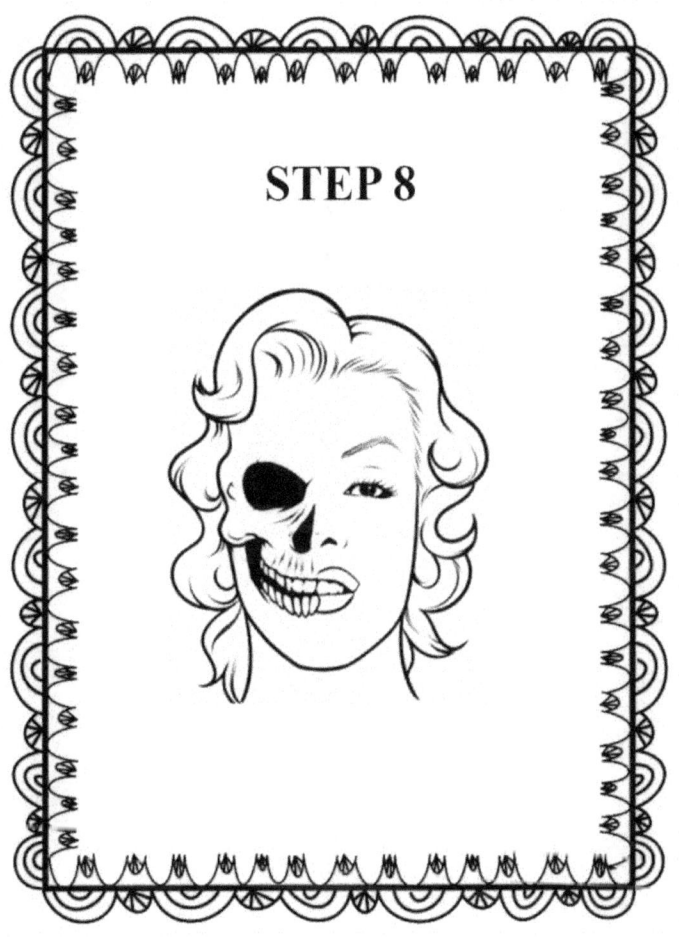

STEP 8

www.ingramcontent.com/pod-product-compliance
Lightning Source LLC
Chambersburg PA
CBHW071642170526
45166CB00003B/1396